Uncle Steve's African Adventure

Steve Bové

Uncle Steve's African Adventure

ISBN-13: 978-1503206908

ISBN-10: 1503206904

This book is dedicated to my nieces and nephew:

Sophia, Olivia, Gabrielle, Alexis and RJ.

One day Uncle Steve and Aunt Jenn decided to go to Africa. They wanted to go on a safari so they could see all the animals that live there.

Africa is far away and Uncle Steve was very tired when they got there. Aunt Jenn was too excited to be sleepy.

She was ready to explore Africa. Their adventure started

in a tiny airport in the middle of the African wilderness.

There was a van waiting for them to take Aunt Jenn to

see her favorite animal – the Giraffe.

The Giraffe was very tall and he wondered what Uncle
Steve had in his hand.

When the Giraffe bent over he saw it was grass. He said

"hello" and ate the grass Uncle Steve brought for him.

Aunt Jenn saw how big the Giraffe was and knew he needed more to eat. "Here you go," she said as she fed him some more grass.

Since there was a lot to see, they got back in the van.

Aunt Jenn saw a sign. "The sign says 'Bumps Ahead,'"

"But it should say 'Monkeys Ahead,'" she yelled!

"Not just Monkeys," said Uncle Steve. "Look it's the

Maasi Warriors doing the 'Lion Dance'."

"Their dance must be working!" he exclaimed. "Over by

the tree is a Lion. It's the King of the Jungle!"

When the Lion saw Uncle Steve and Aunt Jenn he let out

a loud 'ROAR'! Then he turned over and took a nap.

Next Uncle Steve and Aunt Jenn went to visit a Cheetah

and his sister. "The Cheetahs are sleepy too," Uncle

Steve noticed. "It must be nap time for everyone."

"Not for everyone," said Aunt Jenn. "There's a Mommy Elephant with her baby taking a walk."

"And right behind them is their Dad," Uncle Steve said.

"He doesn't look like he wants to play."

"That's ok," said Aunt Jenn. "The Baby Elephant wants
to say hello!"

"So does the Rhinoceros!" shouted Uncle Steve.

After saying hello to the Rhinoceros, they heard a loud THUD. It was very loud but everything was ok, it was just Impalas playing.

Even a little Rainbow Bird heard the commotion. He

looked over to see what was going on.

"Nothing to see here," said the Hippos. They just wanted

to relax in the sun.

They were jealous of the crocodile. He was sound asleep

with his mouth open, snoring and sunning himself.

With everyone relaxing it was strange when Uncle Steve and Aunt Jenn heard footsteps. "Where is everyone going?" they wondered.

"To the river!" shouted Aunt Jenn. "They're thirsty." "So

I am," said Uncle Steve. "But before we go..."

"…We need to say goodbye to our friend the Giraffe."

When the Giraffe heard Uncle Steve and Aunt Jenn were

getting ready to leave, he gave Uncle Steve a big kiss.

"That was funny," giggled Aunt Jenn.

It was time to say goodbye for now. "We'll miss you Giraffe! We'll miss you Africa!" they both shouted as they headed home to get ready for their next adventure.

The End